CW01370447

Be a Success

A Book about Leadership and Being Successful at Work
—With a Partner's Perspective

Stephen and
Jeanette McNamara

Copyright © 2020 Stephen and Jeanette McNamara.

All rights reserved. No part of this book may be reproduced, stored, or transmitted by any means—whether auditory, graphic, mechanical, or electronic—without written permission of the author, except in the case of brief excerpts used in critical articles and reviews. Unauthorized reproduction of any part of this work is illegal and is punishable by law.

ISBN: 978-1-7167-8752-2 (sc)
ISBN: 978-1-7167-8751-5 (e)

Library of Congress Control Number: 2020912702

Because of the dynamic nature of the Internet, any web addresses or links contained in this book may have changed since publication and may no longer be valid. The views expressed in this work are solely those of the author and do not necessarily reflect the views of the publisher, and the publisher hereby disclaims any responsibility for them.

Any people depicted in stock imagery provided by Getty Images are models, and such images are being used for illustrative purposes only. Certain stock imagery © Getty Images.

Lulu Publishing Services rev. date: 07/14/2020

*To our heroes Gary, Bobby, and Louis -
you are our inspiration.*

FOREWORDS

I first met Jeanette in Jordan in 2012 on a charity trek for Help for Heroes. I remember describing Jeanette as a 'pocket rocket,' being petite and always out front on the trek, giving a different meaning to 'leading from the front.'

Jeanette lives for her family and is one of the most giving people I have met. Her strength of character is outstanding, especially with all that life has thrown at her.

Steve and Jeanette are 2 of the kindest and caring people I have met. I wish them every success with this book and their future. They truly deserve it.

Pam Garland

In 2016, I was fortunate enough to follow in the footsteps of Steve McNamara. As I review the draft of his book, I see he has highlighted principles, such as "high-risks first" and "the standard you walk past is the standard you accept," which have endured since Steve began promoting them in 2011. They have endured because they are true, they are simple, and they work.

I've spent a great deal of time and effort studying safety regulations, engineering, and management. However, I've learned, especially from working with Steve, that an essential ingredient for personal success is the practical wisdom that comes from hands-on experiences, such as Steve has, and you will learn about in this book. I highly recommend it for both insight and inspiration.

**Laura P. Cummings, P.E., CSP
Director, Environment, Health, and Safety**

I've been fortunate to work with Steve for years while working on OHS in the same company. Since then, our paths have separated, but the friendship has stayed. Reading his book brought back many memories and lessons shared.

This book challenges you to take the journey into yourself. Not always easy, but definitely worth taking. Reading this book gets you to think, what is important, and how to enforce the good things in life.

Steve truly lives in work life as he writes. He treats people equally and at the same time gives you the feeling that you are unique, a star. I hope that you will take on the challenge and reflect your own way. And I certainly hope that everyone gets to meet their own Steve to give support and encouragement.

I appreciate Jeanette's insight, as I only know Steve from work life. Wise words and commitment as well as firmly keeping the other on the ground. Listening to the views and reflecting them would help so many - both in work and family environment. We need to act together, not against each other. I know, it is hard to stop holding on to your views as well as thinking about work, but also very needed and refreshing.

Giving to others does not mean that you have less yourself.

I recommend you take the time to read and foremost think and strive for change.

Thank you, Steve and Jeanette!

Ulla Juuti
Business Developer, Occupational Safety

CONTENTS

1. Introduction 1
2. How Best to Use This Book? 3
3. So Why You? 5
4. Something about Us..7
5. Success Looks Different to Everyone..11
6. Be Kind, Modest & Understanding 13
7. Leadership...21
8. What is Your Vision? 29
9. What Is Your Plan?.. 33
10. High Risk First 39
11. Build Your Reputation and Standing.. 43
12. Build Your Team and Trust.. 53
13. No Stupid Rules 61
14. The Standard You Walk Past Is The Standard You Accept 67
15. Communication... 73
16. Focus On People at The Front Of The Train............................... 79
17. You Get Out What You Put In 85
18. Worklife balance.. 89
19. Job Interviews.. 93
20. Measure Improvement and Success 97
21. Evolution v Revolution... 99
22. Speed/Numbers v Quality 103
23. How To Deal With Setbacks 109

24. Take a Risk 113
25. Education and training 119
26. Coaching and Mentoring 125
27. Next steps 131
28. Mental Health 135

INTRODUCTION

So what sets this book apart from other paperbacks you might see on the bookstore shelve—What is its unique selling point?

In this book, you are going to get both sides of the story. How I saw it and how Jeanette, my wife saw it! Her sacrifices were far more significant than mine. So you are going to be getting it with "both-barrels." Jeanette will comment and write about her experiences. It has been a team effort, and it is a journey we have both been on together. Without any shadow of a doubt, my work success and our subsequent financial security are because of her sacrifices, support, and guidance.

I am an ordinary everyday person, most likely just like you! These are my observations, examples, strategies, and methods that I have seen work in practice. I have financial security a high level of job satisfaction, and have had excellent career progression, underpinned by a rock-solid supportive family unit.

Jeanette has borne the brunt of all the highs and lows. When I think about the times, I have been away travelling with work to exotic locations, networking, eating good food, and drinking excellent wines. She was the one (often alone) who held everything together, building a solid family foundation usually under extreme pressure.

Anyone who has gone on to be successful will have had to make sacrifices and difficult choices. This book will help you understand the impact and pitfalls, so you are aware and forearmed when these critical decisions arise.

HOW BEST TO USE THIS BOOK?

Jeanette and I were speaking to a younger work colleague of mine (who I always thought had great potential) in the shopping aisle in my local Sainsbury supermarket.

He had recently applied for an internal production management vacancy and unfortunately had not managed to get an interview this time around. He was not sure what to do next and I could see he was disappointed, downhearted, and seeking guidance and support.

This book was written for this type of person and situation in mind.

Once I am happy with the final draft, I am going to point him in the direction of our book. I hope he finds it useful on his journey to success.

This book is for anyone who wants to get on in life, and they could be doing any job role.

My last seven years' employment has been in safety; some of the real-life examples used in the book may reflect this fact.

The main focus is the tools and techniques you might find useful to help you achieve your goals. It is all about taking the best bits of what I have seen, experienced, and learned.

Our aim to help you avoid some of the mistakes and pitfalls that I made, and I have made many! I hope you find it useful, and I would appreciate your feedback.

You should take the opportunity to write inside the book, highlight "golden nuggets," cross out where you disagree, and please feel free to contact me for clarification or further comments. I will put my personal email in the book so you can ask your questions if you wish.

I will try my best to reply to you.

stevemc1965@sky.com

Now let me share with you how I got here and how Jeanette helped me!

SO WHY YOU?

When I think about it, this book is really about leadership. It doesn't matter who you are, your upbringing, or education. I can say with complete confidence, that your style of leadership and personal values will decide how far you go in your work and own life.

Leadership roles can sometimes be very lonely places! It is my sincere hope that this book can help you make good choices and give you the confidence to push on and be successful.

In this book, we will explore, discuss, challenge, and build plans for someone who should be very important in your life. A person because of various reasons, you often put last, you forget to develop, and you don't give enough praise or credit too—*that person is you.*

Although we have written this book, it is 100 percent all about you.

I hope I can give you some small steps and advice to help unlock your full potential, so you can have the success you want for yourself. If this happens to just one person, then this book has been worth writing.

It is great to see people who started at the bottom of the ladder who have worked their way to the top. It is motivating and gives hope to everyone else.

So Why Not You?

You could be an:

operator	apprentice
safety representative	production Manager
supervisor	safety/environmental advisor
shift Manager	safety manager / director
team leader	operations manager

You really can be anyone who is thinking about the next steps.

You are probably someone who is looking for a career move or some real-life, hands-on guidance and practical support on how to progress your career.

You may need help reaching the milestone you set yourself.

You may be looking to achieve an excellent work-life balance.

You may be looking to be successful in leadership and management.

You may be in a rut, have existing baggage, or struggle to get your message across.

You are undoubtedly keen to increase your value in your organization and improve your:

1. Take-home salary.
2. Job security.
3. Career opportunities.

SOMETHING ABOUT US

STEPHEN:

I have been in your shoes, and I have made the same mistakes (most likely more) you have. However, I want you to learn the lessons I have without having to go through the pain I did. I hope this book can help fast track you forward.

Success is within your power; you only need to unlock your potential! I believe I can help you with this!

I work for one of the world's largest paper companies. Currently, I head up the safety and sustainability for a business area (BA) leading teams in the UK, USA, Germany, France, Austria, and Finland.

I have asked real-life people to support and endorse this book. People who have known me for good and bad over many years and with whom I have worked with closely. They have experienced the same struggles at work like you and me, and have gone on to be successful.

I can say, hand on heart, that I love my job and care deeply for the people and the company. I am part of the senior management team in a global company, and I hope I am a respected team member and a leader with credibility at all levels.

I say this not to be big-headed or to boast. I want to show you that if I can do this, then why not you! However, it was not always like this!

I left school at sixteen with almost zero qualifications, and my academic education was not great. I served seven years in the British Military in the Army Air Corps. This environment is where my understanding of leadership qualities and safety standards began.

None of my successes would have been possible without:

1. The support, guidance, and tolerance from Jeanette, my beautiful, amazing, and talented wife.
2. My work colleagues, many of whom I consider close friends. My success is truly about a team effort.
3. The company for seeing my potential before I did and supporting me all the way.
4. Myself, for taking the time to improve through studying and self-development courses, so I was able to fulfill my promise.

One of my main motivations for writing this book was my general frustration when picking up other leadership/safety/management books I often end up very disappointed or deflated. Many of the authors having never worked in a factory environment, never struggled with poor education, or never had to fight from the bottom of the pile.

Very often, it was all management theory, not practical that I could personally relate to endorsed by CEOs of multinationals or other stellar highflying people with limited knowledge of what really goes on in the workplace.

These books felt a million miles away from me and my day to day challenges.

Personal success for me means;

- Having loving, supportive family and friends.

Work success for me is being in:

- A company and job that I thoroughly enjoy. I get massive levels of satisfaction from my job, and I work with a team of people who I trust, respect, and I care deeply about.

This book is not solely my work. It is a collection of ideas and practical advice from many of the inspirational leaders and teams I have had the opportunity to work alongside. It combines all this with my thoughts and opinions on success and failure.

JEANETTE:

Success for me, is the mental and financial wellbeing of my family. There is no point in my mind to have lots of money if you are in a job you don't like, that causes you anxiety, stress, or depression.

What makes me proud is my family doing well, succeeding in whatever they choose to do.

Success has many benefits, which can include a better monetary way of life and extra opportunities. This extra money can bring with it travel, beautiful houses, cars, etc.

There can be a negative cost of success. Too often relationships breakdown the person you are with changes in front of your eyes. Unfortunately, he or she can't always see it happening! The money is good. However, beautiful cars, houses and holidays do not compensate for the loss of other more essential things in our lives.

Your partner being away often and missing important milestones like birthdays and anniversaries—*What value and cost do you put on time and personal commitment?*

We scrimped and saved at the beginning of our marriage. Our financial state and our relationship have now positively changed due to our effort and perseverance. It has been tough at times, but it was worth it.

SUCCESS LOOKS DIFFERENT TO EVERYONE

Let me try and explain what I mean I was recently in the back of a Helsinki taxi heading toward Vantaa Airport for my regular Friday early morning flight home. The taxi driver had a very open personality, and we immediately started chatting.

She told me a fascinating story about herself. Not so long ago, she was an account manager earning a good salary. However, she was overworked, stressed, and had grown to dislike her job. The worry from working in this high-stress environment was making her ill.

Her real passion in life has always been photography. So against all the advice of her family, friends, and work colleagues, she resigned from her job. She now drives a taxi to meet people and earn extra money; she has started her own photography business, and she is building this business day by day.

It is hard work, and she is often short of money. That said, she recently won a significant commission to hang one of her photographs in the suite of the Hotel Royal Evian, a five-star hotel near Lake Geneva, France. She is now her own boss and the master of her own destiny. She has never been happier. This is success for her.

What a truly amazing, brave, and inspirational woman. I was so glad I got into her taxi that morning—so much so that I knew I would have to use her story in this book.

It's your life, so you decide what success is for you!

BE KIND, MODEST & UNDERSTANDING

Let me say the further up the promotion ladder you get, the more tempting it is to become full of your self-importance. Maybe dismissive and sometimes even arrogant, forgetting the person you once were! It really pains me to admit that I became like that many years ago!

I know from experience you can achieve so much more by kind supportive words than being the hard-faced leader.

There is nothing wrong with being ruthless!!

Be Ruthless in:

- *Your own planning.*
- *Your own execution.*
- *Your own follow up.*
- *The standard you set yourself.*

Don't be ruthless in how you deal and interact with people – you are going to be firm when needed (you are not a pushover). You are never ruthless.

A saying that my father regularly uses:

Be careful of whom you stand on in your climb up the ladder; you never know who you will meet on the way down.

Some pointers and advise that have stood me in good stead that I would like to share with you:

- *Never take credit for anyone else's work* - A Motto that sticks with me today from one of my most respected mentors (Capt A.N Moore AAC) from my early days in the Army:

    "When the sun shines, it shines on everyone."

    I remember in the late 90's sitting in a high-level meeting with a hundred plus people. My Manager at the time presented some work we had done together.

    This combined effort was presented at the time as their work.

    I was devastated and very upset! I made a vow never to do that to any person I worked with in the future.

<u>Always</u> give open and public praise to the person who has done the work. To do otherwise is a great opportunity missed. Just imagine highlighting someone's talents within your team and highlighting yours as a leader to allow that talent to flourish.

- *Have courage* – praise your team in the good times and be brave enough to take the pain when things are not going so well.

- *Be courteous* – you get so much more by being polite. Always shake hands, look him or her in the eye and say thank you. That is a powerful tool to have in your armoury.

- *Always reply to emails* – even if it is just a simple thank you, or I will get back to you later on this. Think how frustrating it is for you when you never hear anything back when you email your boss. Why would it be any different for the teams you lead?

- *Stand up for others* – Be brave, stand up for what is right. Treat all people you meet with respect and care.

- *Talk to people Face-to-Face* – do not manage people from behind a desk. Email and phones are great. However, nothing beats taking the time and having a face-to-face conversation where you can read someone's body language and facial expressions. Without a doubt, this is an investment involving time and effort. However, people will respect and appreciate this level of commitment.

- *Help and support people whenever you can* – One day when you need support, someone will probably step forward for you. I always get a huge buzz when I know I have made a difference by helping someone.

- *Keep your sense of humour* – smile, work, and life can be tough enough do not be the person who never has the time to say a kind word to anyone. Do not use offensive language.

- *Reward and recognition* – Recognise your team and individual successes. Reward and recognise good work, good behaviour, and great ideas whenever possible.

- *Trust your instinct* – if something feels wrong, then it probably is wrong. It might also be an opportunity for you to step forward and help.

- *Mentor and coach your team* – take the opportunity to have quality one on one time with your team members. Help and guide them to be successful too.

- *Emotional intelligence* – continually improve, develop, and deploy your softer skill sets, empathy, humility, and caring for your team. I honestly believe these will get you further than any academic qualification, and we will also discuss this further in the chapter on Leadership.

- *Own your mistakes* – if you have made a "cock-up" or had an error of judgment. Then be honest, put your hands up, and take responsibility. I believe most people I have ever worked with value this trait rather than trying to "pass the buck" or keeping the mistake hidden.

Keep your feet on the ground:

Some years ago, my wife told me my attitude and personality were changing. That was tough to hear. However, on reflection over the next few days/ weeks, I knew she was 100 percent right.

Let me give you a simple example; I had my Airline gold card strapped to my travel bags. I was always first on the plane, and I would sometimes walk past people who I could have assisted.

In my mind, I had become an important person!

I can honestly say having that frank and difficult conversation with my wife was one of the best things that could have happened to me.

As a result of this, I believe I am a kinder, caring, and more thoughtful person today.

Remember: No person is indispensable!

Put your hands in a bucket of water, and when you remove it, look and see the big hole you have left, unknown.

Be Kind—if you have nothing nice to say, then say nothing, *Alice Roosevelt Longworth.*

I would like to share a very personal story of how a random act of kindness touched my life and made such an impression on me that it will last my lifetime. I had just flown to Malaysia with work, and on arrival in Kaula Lumpa, I had multiple voicemails from Jeanette explaining that we had a very serious family emergency, and I needed to return home immediately. I waited at the airport and caught the first available return flight home.

After thirty-six hours with no sleep, I finally arrived back at Manchester airport very tired, disorientated, stressed, and emotional. So much so that I walked out from the baggage reclaim area in tears. It had been a very tough two days, and I was completely exhausted. One of the local airport taxi drivers approached me and asked me if I was okay and if he could help in any way. He was a different ethnicity and religion to me, which makes this story and the help he gave more moving to me. *He turned out to be a true gentleman and a truly extraordinary person!*

After telling him my problems, he insisted that he drive me the 120 miles to my home address a 240 mile round trip for himself, he stayed with me and supported me in my greatest hour of need. As we got talking, he explained about his own family and the mental health struggles his family had also been through. *Unbelievably, he was in my position five years before our fateful meeting!*

Most humbling of all, he would not take one penny for payment even though he had lost a day's work and used a significant amount of petrol. *I honestly believe he was my guardian angel that day, and he will never know how much his random act of kindness touched me and helped me.* If I can be half the man he is, then I will be doing well.

JEANETTE:

One story I would like to tell as a word of caution for you all is; as Stephen moved up the promotion ladder, he started becoming self-centered and selfish. It got to such an issue that I sat down with him and explained I didn't like the person he was turning into.

If he didn't change, then, in all honesty, our marriage was on a cliff-edge. That conversation was a turning point in our relationship, and I am thankful to say it had a positive impact on him. He has definitely gone back to the loving kinder person I married.

I am convinced that this was learned behaviour as he was role modeling the actions of people around him and how they behaved.

There is still one person who I call "God," as in my opinion, they seemed to think they were exactly that! I honestly believe Stephen was trying to emulate this person. He didn't need to. I always knew he had the ability and capability to do it his own way. So there was never any need in my eyes for him to try and copy or role-model someone else.

Always be your own person.

I often talk about "givers and takers" in my experience, one person in a relationship seems to give more than the other. The taker can take without realising the impact of their actions on the other person.

I believe there are givers and takers in every relationship.

If there are two takers, then I don't believe the relationship will work long-term.

So what I am trying to advise is, you have to try and strike the right balance, don't just take all the time or one day you will find the pot will be empty!

I won't be too negative about how hard Stephen has worked to get where he is today. It has been a journey of highs and lows. We have both had to work hard to make it work, and enjoy what we have today.

QUESTION:

When did you last help someone in need?

When did you last stand up for someone?

Have you ever taken credit for anyone's work?

If yes, how could you have managed this situation differently?

LEADERSHIP

Firstly don't worry - You can learn to be a good leader.

Remember, "A leader is a dealer in HOPE!" ~ Napoléon Bonaparte

One of my favourite jobs in the British Army was The Commanding Officers (CO) driver come bodyguard. He was the most senior person in our Regiment and held all the reins of power. In Germany during the mid-1980s, these senior ranking officers were high-value targets for many terrorist organisations, so you had to be somewhat switched on to do this job role.

I would be with this person for a minimum of four hours a day; I learned how to communicate with senior people in the Military, for example, when to talk, when to listen and when to shut up. It was an invaluable experience for my future progression. I remember one particular occasion when I was on a disciplinary charge for getting into trouble, and the CO had to deliver my punishment. That evening I had to drive him home and take care of his personal safety.

I will always remember his words of wisdom; L/CPL McNamara:

- Never hold a grudge.
- Use this disappointment to learn and better yourself.

- Think about how you need to behave if you want success in the future.

The CO never swore, lost his temper, or compromised his values or beliefs. On the day I left the Army, although, at this point in my career, we had not seen each other for two years, he took the time to phone me up and wish me good luck for the future. Now that is a great leader in my eyes.

To be a good leader, you cannot just have academic intelligence; you also need emotional intelligence.

Let me explain:

- You need the skills to be able to deal with people and everyday life.
- You have to be able to navigate different situations and surroundings.
- You have to be able to connect with people and speak in a language they can understand.

Therefore having emotional intelligence, I would rate as highly (if not more highly) as having academic intelligence. I have known some super-intelligent people who have had great difficulty in leading teams or fitting into everyday work situations.

One of the most successful military organisations in the world is the British Army, which has over three hundred years of history. They invest heavily in teaching emotional intelligence, learning how to be an effective and inspirational leader.

Having been part of this program from sixteen years old, I know it takes time, and you need:

- Self-motivation.
- Practice.
- Constructive feedback.

So don't despair if you do not have a good educational background; we discuss this later in the book. However, if you have people skills and can communicate and motivate, you are halfway there already.

Of course, the goal is to blend both academic and emotional leadership, so you become a more rounded and complete package.

A great example of leadership told to me by my son:

AFGHANISTAN 2012

- A team of the United Kingdom (UK) Royal Engineers (RE) was getting ready to clear a large compound of Improvised Explosive Devices (IED).

- The team of Royal Engineers led by a Sergent and consisted of five junior ranked soldiers.

- A little further back was approximately one hundred NATO soldiers waiting to go into the compound to carry out an intelligence-led search.

- The NATO soldiers led by an officer who outranked the (UK) Royal Engineers Sergent were understandably nervous and impatient to get on with the task in hand.

- The NATO officer started applying pressure onto the lower-ranked Royal Engineer Sergent to get the bomb search done more quickly.

- At this point, under immense pressure, the Sergent could have buckled and started getting his team to speed up, maybe take short cuts, putting them all in grave danger.

- The Sergent didn't flinch, passing the Valon (Metal detecting device) to the higher ranking NATO Officer. Then politely asking if they thought they could do the job better or quicker, please feel free to give it a try.

- Otherwise, it was best to let the Royal Engineer IED search team do the work as trained so everyone can go home safely.

- Can you imagine the amount of respect you would have for this Sergent if they were your team leader at that moment in time?

The Sergent put the welfare and wellbeing of his team above everything else, and at a time, he was under immense pressure. On that day, he made sure his team went home safely. What an inspiration for others to emulate. Be brave—it can be a lonely place being a leader

Leaders Must ~*Mark Pollard:*

- Strive for excellence.
- Create continuous forward momentum.
- Drive change.
- Adapt style and technique.

Always lead by example and don't ask people to do a task; you would not be prepared to do yourself.

Leaders Values ~*Mark Pollard:*

- Say Thank You, we all need to be appreciated.
- Listen to people, engage, and consult your team.
- Always be honest.
- Respect the people around you.
- Build trust.
- Give everyone a fair chance.

If you are a leader at some point, you will have to lead; the clue is definitely in the title.

Leadership is not a natural trait in everyone, so I will take this opportunity to share some attributes of good leaders I have worked with:

- Positive.
- Consistent and fair.
- Good role model and mentors.
- Walk the talk.
- Strong values and beliefs.
- Brave and held up their hands when they made a mistake.
- They took the time to listen to your point of view.

When I am doing any training, I always ask this question;

Think of a leader/teacher/mentor in your life who you admired. What attributes did they have that gained your respect and admiration. The answers I have received over many years are always almost the same. When I think of my most inspirational leader My Officer Commanding (OC) Capt A N Moore AAC this is what I would write;

- Honest.
- Firm.
- Trustworthy.
- Challenged you to do better.
- Role model.
- Never took the easy route.
- Led by example.
- Caring.
- Inspiring.
- Listened to you and gave you time.

I believe we should strive to have the same attributes as the people who positively influenced and inspired us as we muddled our way through life.

On the flip-side, I am sure we can all remember the leaders who were bullies, angry, ungrateful, and left you feeling frightened or distressed.

A short word on making decisions and being decisive—Indecision can be so frustrating for many people, therefore:

- If you are unable to make a decision, immediately take the time to consider, seek advice, or reflect on what your choice will mean / outcome?
- Let people know what and why you are taking this course of action.
- Don't be rushed into making the wrong decision equally do be aware of not making any decision at all, or taking to long to come to any conclusion—*This trait can is often viewed as a significant flaw or weakness.*

We are going to focus on the positive and role-model ourselves on the best leaders we know. These inspiring people, although they probably will never know it have left legacies that last a generation.

QUESTION:

Name three Role Models in your life?

What attributes would you like to develop in yourself that they had in abundance?

What are your leadership strengths?

What are your leadership weaknesses?

WHAT IS YOUR VISION?

The first step you have to take to an improved future is being able to envision it—how do you know where you want to get to if you cant see it!

What does success look like to you?

We are all different; how you view success will not be the same as others see it.

It might be a promotion, a career change, a salary increase, or job satisfaction. Whatever it is, it is your view of success and personal to you. I am sure that it will develop and change over time.

One of the critical moments in my working life was when I sat down and thought long and hard about where I wanted to get too. What was my aim and vision for the next three to five years? Then I wrote it down.

The simple act of writing my vison down for me was a revelation.

It made me realise that the job I was currently doing (Shift Manager), the one I had worked for five years to achieve, was not what I wanted to do long term.

After being in the role less than twelve months, I desired a new challenge! However, I had not seen this until it was in front of my eyes in black and white. Now it was tangible, and for the first time in my life, I had a real idea where I wanted to get too.

Some of the questions I started asking myself as a result were:

1. What does success look like for me?
2. What am I striving for when it comes to my work?
3. What do I need to do?
4. How can I help the company succeed?
5. How do I motivate all the people I work with, so they succeed too?
6. Where do my family and personal life sit in this vision?

I will take this opportunity to share one of my earlier Visions. I first started using them over fifteen years ago. I can honestly say this has helped keep me motivated and focused since I started writing this information down.

I want to show you how simple my vision was—*Why can't yours be as simple as this?*

My early-years vision:

1. A company Director or General Manager within five years.
2. Retire before I am sixty.
3. Be Financially Secure.
4. Home and Worklife in Balance.
5. Maintain a Good Level of Health and Fitness.

A vision is straightforward to put down onto paper; we all have ambitions, dreams, and hopes for ourselves.

The hard part is putting a plan together that will make your vision turn into reality, and we will discuss this as we progress.

When I gained promotion to a director level, I hit my primary goal several years after putting this simple vision together.

Let me show you what I mean when I say a vision is straightforward to write down. If I were to think of the England Men's football team, my vision would be:

1. FIFA World Cup Champions.
2. UEFA Euro Champions.
3. In the top three of the FIFA world rankings.
4. An England player wins FIFA Player of The Year.

If I think of my work colleagues from Finland with their obsession/passion with ice hockey, my vision for them might be something like this:

1. Winter Olympics – Gold Medal.
2. Ice hockey world championships – Gold Medal.
3. Ranked the number one Ice Hockey Team in the world.
4. To beat Sweden.

The vision sets the scene. It is personal to me, and if it involves work, it should be relevant to the organisation where I am looking to make a positive impact.

It must excite you and motivate you to achieve more!

Now having shown all of the above, you need a realistic and focussed plan to make your vision a reality.

WHAT IS YOUR PLAN?

Why leave your success to luck, chance, or someone else?

It is your life! Take ownership and take control of your own destiny; you may only get one shot at this.

- Know what you want long term.
- Know what you want short term.

The plan is the hard part! Firstly keep it simple, realistic, and achievable. I always remember my colleague and good friend from Finland (thank you, Sari) favourite sayings: *"Keep it Simple Stupid" (the stupid often replaced by her with my name Steve)* —I am not sure if it was her saying, but it has always worked well for me.

Your plan is a tangible, measurable, and more detailed set of priorities. That, if implemented with a high degree of urgency and quality, will deliver your vision.

This plan is the foundation of your future success.

Focus on the delivery and execution, i.e.,

- Do what you are meant to do.
- Do it when you are meant to do it.

- *No excuses or maybes.*

My Plan: This was my work plan to achieve the vision I laid out in my previous chapter.

ROLES	NEEDS	SKILLS
Manage the dept to fulfill its maximum potential	Ongoing leadership training on how to successfully manage high performing teams	We have good trainers in-house. Identify our best trainers and get them engaged - people who thrive on a challenge.
Review and measure targets and goals	Train our teams to understand process capability fully	Engage our Continual Improvement to train our teams in SPC charts and continual improvement
Ensure the dept meets the customer's requirements	Train our teams to understand the customer fully	organise customer visits for all levels of our teams
Get the best from our suppliers	understand our suppliers and their limitations	Be Patient/ change will not come quicker - the plan is good
Ensure the dept works safely	Safety given the highest priority	Train leaders and operators in safety - good quality training
Get the best out of our team and challenge old ways of thinking	safe environment and team working - Train to look after each other	Involve the team and communicate very well - regular weekly and quarterly team meetings
Champion and support the whole dept	Understand different styles and other dept viewpoints	Open mind

Make sure within your plan; there are no "stupid rules." No own goals, objectives, or targets that are impossible to achieve. Stretched targets are a must. However, impossible ones just turn people off.

Both vision & plan: Today, in my mind, are straightforward - I hope you agree it does not get much easier than what I have just shown!

- Remember - Enthusiasm and Success are contagious

Another benefit of this simple approach (vision & plan) is it gives you the power to communicate effectively at all levels. You can do this communication with confidence and without any fear or hesitation because you know the vision and plan intimately; after all, it is your or your teams' idea.

This whole journey is all about engaging people, motivating them, and turning them on!

PLAN B

Don't be afraid to change direction if it is clear your plan is not working or delivering the results you anticipated and communicated. I have seen many people lose their jobs or shifted sideways as a result of rigidly sticking with a plan that is clearly not working—when everyone else knows the plan is doomed.

Be agile and flexible in your thinking, and have a Plan B in your mind or back pocket, you might never need it. However, it is ready just in case you do.

That said, you are not going to change just because it is getting hard. There will be highs and lows on this journey, and you are going to have to learn to tough it out. You will have to understand the times when it is just a problematic patch, and you work through this, and when your plan is failing—no one said this journey was going to be easy.

To summarise, Plan and Vision explain the journey you are going on, how to get there, and what success looks like when you ultimately arrive.

JEANETTE:

I am going to keep it very simple and get straight to the point here – don't forget your family and loved ones in your vision and plan.

I can't think of anyone more important than them when it comes to my happiness and success—so why would you not include them too.

Don't let them be an afterthought or always be second-best; if they are important to you too, then put them "front and center" of what you do.

One day your children will have grown up and left home you don't want to look back with regret thinking about the time you could have spent with them or the missed family opportunities – so plan for them too.

QUESTION:

What is Your Vision?

What is Your Plan?

What Do You Want for Yourself?

What is Stopping You?

HIGH RISK FIRST

In most companies, it is not possible to do everything that needs doing all at the same time, so you are going to have to prioritise.

It doesn't matter what job role you do; it should always be High Risks first. High Risks are a fundamental component of any action plan, be it for productivity, quality, cost-saving, environmental or safety, etc. High Risk means identifying any gaps that will cause severe failure or consequences. I.e., you focus on the critical issues and push more minor issues to the back of the queue.

For example,

> I recently attended an excellent work summit, where I wrote down eight pages of what I thought was inspiring and great ideas.
>
> Could you then imagine me then going back to my organisation and overwhelming them with my eight pages of these great thoughts and ideas!
>
> What I did was narrow down eight pages to four High Risk ideas we could consider—and even then, I knew my boss might reduce these four down to two ideas.

Whenever I have moved jobs, led a safety improvement program, or taken new responsibility, I have always prioritised the High Risks above everything else.

For clarification, this does not mean that we forget about the minor or lesser problem. However, you are very focussed, and the priority always goes to High Risk.

TOP 5 RISKS

What are the top five risks that are under your direct control?

You may have many more in number than this. However, on your notice board or your desk, I would recommend that you have these "top five" clearly displayed so that these are never out of your sight or mind.

My top five risks today are:

1. Risk assessment quality.
2. People not following the rules.
3. Leaders taking responsibility and being good role models.
4. Quality of training provision.
5. Quality and number of audits carried out.

Like I have already said, it does not have to be safety-related. You can use this approach for any area of your responsibility.

The positive outcome of taking this type of approach is a reduction in your exposure to something significant going wrong. In essence, the kind of situations that can get people hurt, fired, cause a loss of reputation or orders. Therefore, you can manage the small everyday problems that always come along.

INFLUENCE V CONCERN

"Focus on what you can control, and do not waste energy on the things you cannot" ~ unknown.

Let me try and explain, today, accidents at home are a hot topic in most companies and are having a real negative impact on work absentee rates. Subsequently, there is pressure on many businesses to help people make the right safety decisions outside of working hours.

- Is this something I am concerned about – Yes (but not my No1 priority).

- Is this something I can Influence – Maybe (most likely not)?

Your time and effort, in this instance, is most likely best used by stopping people from working unsafely at work. This more focussed work safety approach is where you can make a real impact that may indirectly result in more awareness in the home.

Working on low influence, low concern topics like accidents at home might be a hindrance to you in reaching the vision and targets you have set yourself.

Focus on areas where you have the biggest influence and the most significant concerns and build these into your plan—Don't be distracted or diverted by everyday routine work.

QUESTION:

What are your High Risks?

What are your most significant concerns?

What are you working on today that are low influence and low concern issues?

Why are you working on these low influence and low concern issues?

BUILD YOUR REPUTATION AND STANDING

Let us talk about you; I believe It is almost entirely within your own hands how you are perceived, respected, and valued as a person.

Firstly, enjoy what you are doing and smile often.

The aim of this chapter is for you to understand that:

- You have the tools and techniques to build a trusting and open relationship with the people you come into contact with—i.e., your boss(es), the people who report to you, and your peers.

- People see the value you and your team members bring to the organization.

- You don't judge on first impressions, gossip, and past mistakes you are going to give people the chance to show their value and worth.

"A leopard can't change its spots" I still often hear this saying as justification for writing people off or dismissing them for past mistakes.

When I think back to my early days at work, I feel a sense of disappointment in the way I was sometimes perceived. I am absolute proof that you can change and that you can change people's opinions of you.

I remain in contact with many of the people from my younger days, and I always use myself as a positive role model - to show that you do not need to be defined by the past mistakes you made. You can continuously improve your current situation if you have the willingness to do so.

Let me give an example of what I mean, S was an operator who had a bit of a "reputation," S was vocal, and could be a bit difficult to manage. S was an informal leader and an influencer in the blue-collar workforce.

I was looking to strengthen and support the leadership structure in my organization, and as a result, we were planning to create four new leadership positions.

I asked S to apply for one of the vacancies, after a long and open discussion. S made the brave decision and applied. I have to say when I commented that I wanted to give S a chance, many of my close leadership team thought I might be making a mistake.

Some observations:

- S didn't let me down.
- I never regretted making this decision.
- S took the opportunity, and over many years proved the doubters wrong.
- S worked hard as they knew I had taken a personal risk in selecting them for advancement.
- We both had an emotional stake in making this appointment work.

Although S has now left the company I currently work for, we remain firm friends, and we both often referrer to that day I gave him/ her the opportunity when others wrote him/ her off.

One challenge in building your reputation is to show you can effectively lead your team and deliver the required results be this in safety or any other skill or expertise.

You are going to have a positive outlook; you are optimistic even during the most challenging times. When you highlight or find a problem, you bring a solution at the same time.

- No one wants to work with negative "glass always half empty" type of person—They just suck the life and energy out of the room.

You are going to need to keep your feet on the ground and head out of the clouds. You can do this by listening and speaking to people at the bottom and top of the organisation and treating all levels equally, i.e., *get out and talk to people, find out what is really going on. This comment is an ongoing theme throughout the book, and I make no apologies for repeating.*

You are going to work hard to develop your empathy and listening skills.

As we will discuss, you are definitely not the person bringing stupid rules into the organisation—You are going to be the one to help remove stupid rules.

Before I forget, you are not the person who asks the stupid questions in company meetings.

Do not believe the person hosting the meeting when they say, "there are no stupid questions." There is always someone who asks a stupid question—*as I have already said, it is not going to be you!*

You have worked hard to build your reputation and credibility, so do not throw this away lightly. Its quickly done yet very hard to build back up again.

You are going to be:

- A good leader and a safe pair of hands.
- Credible.
- Committed.
- Approachable.
- Contactable.
- Knowledgeable.
- A team player.
- A good timekeeper.

You get things done, have common sense, and can relate to all levels in the organization.

You speak the language of the company, and you understand its capabilities and needs.

You keep your meetings short on time, high on quality.

You keep your promises.

You can blend the inspirational—the new ways of thinking with practical hands-on ways of working.

An example I would like to use to illustrate my points, and I could have used this example in several other chapters:

> Some years ago, I was taking part in an external Safety Audit with a person from a different company for ease of explanation lets call this person Peter.
>
> Peter was unconventional, provocative, and had very rigid ideas about how to do safety. It was either right or wrong.
>
> He was a persuasive, active communicator with a straightforward style.
>
> If I am honest, his standing within his organisation was not very good. Although it was clear to me, he was a reasonable, decent person.
>
> As it happened, we paired up together to review chemical safety.
>
> I have to say because of the reputation he had for being complicated and inflexible. I was more worried about working with Peter than the actual review itself.

That said, this audit turned out to be a cornerstone in my understanding of why some people ultimately make it, and others don't.

> During the safety audit, Peter found a household bleach in a toilet that did not have a chemical safety data sheet.
>
> - *In his opinion,* this was now a significant problem and was a clear sign that the organisation was failing in its chemical management processes.

- This problem needed feeding back to the management team in the strongest terms.

- *In my opinion*, this finding was a low risk; it was a household bleach low volume found in a toilet. So it was worth mentioning but not necessarily a big deal. After all, I have the same bleach in my bathroom at home with no Safety Data Sheet—You most likely do too?

Now you think about the organisation we were auditing and to whom we were going to feedback.

- They had been on a two-year safety journey and had made many useful improvements.

- They were looking for feedback to help them take the next steps.

- They understood that they had many minor issues still unresolved. However, their focus and efforts had been on controlling High Risks.

- They certainly wanted to know what high risks were uncontrolled that might seriously harm their people.

I was adamant we must not feed this finding back as a major non-conformity. If we had, then our credibility in this organisation would have been zero.

If we had made a big issue of a minor problem, we could have ruined two years of hard work for no material gain. To clarify, if this had been a High-Risk finding, then, of course, the organisation would have welcomed this feedback in the strongest terms. I am adamant knowing the organisation we were auditing as I did, they would have taken immediate action to remedy the situation.

I subsequently learnt that Peter left his company some six months after this audit. I was saddened but not surprised to hear this news.

A few years later, I joined this organisation to head up safety. They knew me from participating in this OHS audit and appreciated my style and approach.

Sometimes you have to think about the bigger picture and how you can help motivate teams to do better.

The best advice I can give anyone is: *Be Credible.*

A final thought to reflect on:

Get out and talk to people:

> *I can promise you that no one I have ever known who today are respected, and trusted leaders built this reputation from sitting behind a desk. Or by sending a great email or making a good phone call.*

JEANETTE:

Stephen is very focused on what he wants to achieve and does not usually let anything stand in his way. This approach and single-mindedness have been great for his career. On a family relationship level, it has sometimes made me feel like I am stood on the outside looking inwards, often feeling a bit of a "spare part"!

It wasn't good having to wait for him to enjoy what he/ we have achieved. My advice to him has always been to slow down, enjoy life, and appreciate what you have now instead of wanting more.

I can see he is great at building teams at work, and he has an open, friendly style of communication. People always warm to him and like him. I would advise anyone reading this book to work equally, if not harder, on your reputation and standing at home.

There are four people in our relationship; they are me, Stephen, family, and work. The only thing I really want is time, laughter, love, and affection.

Money has never been top of my list. Many of the people Stephen has worked with over the years are money and career orientated. I have to say most are unfortunately divorced and unhappy!

Work hard to not bring your bad day at work home into the family environment.

Enjoy the simple things in life: Always make time to do the little things together; these are really important to me. Therefore, spend quality time with the family, walk the dogs, chat, laugh, and, most importantly, always try to be kind to each other.

QUESTION:

Have you good credibility in your organisation?

Why have you answered, Yes or No?

If the answer is **no**, how can you change this perception?

BUILD YOUR TEAM AND TRUST

My goal has always been for any team that I have led is; they are able to develop their knowledge, skills, ability, and credibility to a level that should I ever move onto a new challenge, the organisation would seriously consider promoting from within rather than hire from the outside.

Thanks to Matti a good friend from Finland for reminding me that; you should build your team so that your subordinates are more talented than you in certain topics.

A leader's task is to create the big picture and also raise subordinates to grow in their career path

In my experience, trust is the foundation for everything you want to do—It is hard to build and easily lost.

Remember, everyone can make a mistake—Everyone can make more than one mistake.

You are entering some of the most exciting and also frightening times as you start sharing your vision and plan with your teams.

You are going to trust them with your innermost thoughts (your hopes and dreams) and ideas. It is like letting someone hold your baby for the first time or something that is equally most precious to you. Of course, you are scared, and you might even be vulnerable. However, you cannot make these crucial journeys to success alone— It is almost always a team effort.

At some point when it comes to sharing your vision and plan with whomever you decide, you are going to have to take a leap of faith, a step into the dark, and ultimately trust your instincts:

- You hope to get meaningful feedback.
- You might get better ideas.
- You are beginning to forge a relationship with your team members based on sharing, trust, and respect.
- It might go wrong. However, don't let the fear of failure stop you from trying.

If you have judged correctly and your instincts have not deserted you (why would they), you will develop a team vision and plan everyone can all get behind. Great News It is no longer your plan; instead, it is *our* plan, and from now on you will:

- Talk to and involve your team.
- Give meaningful opportunities.
- Trust them to deputise (entirely) in your absence and to make decisions.
- Respect and nurture them.
- Highlight their talents and abilities.
- Reward and recognise.
- Be open with them whenever possible.
- Make it personal and share your experiences.
- Listen when they are talking.

- Help them when needed.
- Be visible, approachable, and contactable.
- Coach and mentor them.
- Be prepared to back your team when they are in the right.
- Always say thank you.

Some further advice I would like to suggest; don't drive your people too hard; you get further with a light touch and support. I have never been someone that emotionally or mentally breaks people or teams. I believe you get the best out of people by removing fear and building them up, not knocking them down.

Don't micromanage; the best results I have ever seen are from teams that are allowed to work within a framework with the authority to make decisions. Let me explain:

I once managed a team that held a global production record for continuous operation without stopping. This 72-hour record remained unbroken for many years.

My small role in this record was to provide the framework for the manager and operators under my control to be as effective as possible, i.e.;

- Budgets and operational support for;
    - Manning.
    - Training.
    - Tools and equipment.
    - Customer orders.
    - Time for toolbox talks and departmental meetings.

The operators doing the actual job on the production machinery had full authority for:

- All aspects of safety.
- The deployment of the manning.
- The quality of the customer orders.
- The best use of the tools and equipment.
- The workflow and production speed.

The worst thing I could have done when we all knew that we were getting close to breaking the existing production record, and there was a real buzz of excitement across the whole organization, would have been to try and micro-manage this type of situation. After all, that is why we have leadership structures in place!

You provide the framework so success can happen, and you have to trust all your team to deliver.

Remember: "When the sun shines, it shines on everyone."

It was a great feeling to be able to thank the team for this fantastic achievement. Knowing that by me standing back and not interfering, I had helped this happen.

You are going to delegate authority, not responsibility.

I was recently watching "The Apprentice" on BBC television where the anchor of the show came out with a great statement:

> *The art of a good manager is if you are not as good as someone else, let the someone else do it!*

What a great suggestion the question is, are you brave enough to let someone else do it if they can do better?

STRENGTHS AND WEAKNESSES

Everybody has strengths and weaknesses; no one person is the finished article. Know your and your team's strengths and weaknesses. Try to ensure you have a good range and balance of personalities and skillsets within your team.

Try to avoid having a team where you are all the same personality type or have similar strengths and weaknesses. You are setting yourself up for failure. You are trying to have the right blend and balance, so you complement and challenge each other to succeed.

Support, coach, and mentor your weaker members when needed. Help develop people who want more to achieve their aims and ambitions.

JEANETTE:

Stephen has a very open nature and would always want to trust someone and give them an opportunity rather than not give them a chance in the first place.

I am definitely of a different character and midset than Stephen, and before I would open up and let someone get to close, they would need to prove their trustworthiness to me.

As you can see, we are both like chalk and cheese—both very different in our outlooks and approaches.

If I were ultra-critical, I would say that sometimes Stephen gives to much away, and he is to open with his teams. He trusts them to the extent that he is very honest about his work and personal plans, and they often know much more about him than he does about them.

However, this honest and open approach has served him very well. I know that he is very successful in leading teams, implementing important projects, and people openly ask to work with him as they value his style of leadership and the trust and teamwork that he instills within his teams.

With all that said, I don't think there is a right or wrong way when it comes to trust and building effective teams; it is just a different way. With both ways carrying benefits and risks

You just need to work out what is your own unique style one that you feel comfortable with and one that will work well for you.

QUESTION:

How are you going to build trust within your team?

Who don't you trust, and why is this?

What can you do to change this situation?

What meaningful tasks can you delegate to your team where they have authority?

What are your strengths and weaknesses?

What is your plan to improve?

NO STUPID RULES

You are going to help remove stupid rules, not bring them.

I believe one of the biggest problems we have in safety today is our credibility and image. We have sometimes made worse when we continue to enforce or make "Stupid Rules."

These are rules not usually followed, mainly when managers or leaders are not present— everyone knows they are stupid rules, but no one is brave enough to remove or replace them.

I will share a couple of examples of stupid rules:

Stupid Rule Example 1:

A factory location has one department with high levels of noise. For ease of supervision and safety enforcement, it is mandatory for all employees throughout the whole factory location to wear hearing protection irrespective of the actual noise level risk in their own departments.

This rule includes people working in the dispatch area where the noise levels are minimal who drive electric forklift trucks.

The people driving the electric forklifts are under scrutiny, due to non-compliance with the mandatory safety rule.

There is no legal requirement for hearing protection to be worn in the dispatch area—it is just a factory-wide rule and seen as a stupid rule at that!

It would be safer for the drivers to be able to hear what is going on around them when driving.

The people driving the electric forklifts think this is a "Stupid Rule" that impedes safety not improves it.

They are now at risk of severe disciplinary action as a result of not following the rules.

Maybe the answer is as simple as this:

- Identify the area where hearing protection is mandatory
- Provide the correct equipment and training.
- Ensure anyone entering the high noise area follows the mandatory rule.
- Remove this mandatory blanket (stupid rule) requirement for areas not affected.
- Coach and mentor your leaders, so they have the confidence to lead.
- *Do not use a safety rule as a substitute for leadership it will ultimately fail as in this example just shown*

Stupid Rule Example 2 (reproduced below with the kind permission of the BBC & BBC News Website):

I was delighted to read on the BBC News that many Airlines are working on removing a "Stupid Rule." A rule that anyone who has ever flown would have thought and known about; why do we board the airplane front first?

Gatwick trial cuts plane boarding time by 10%

The frustration of waiting for someone to put their bag in an overhead locker may soon be over if a test to get people on planes quicker is successful.

Gatwick says it is working with EasyJet to try out new ways to board passengers at the London airport.

They include boarding people in window seats first, starting at the back, followed by middle then aisle. Gatwick said different boarding methods could reduce the journey from the airport gate to seat by about 10%.

The airport operator says that the window-to-aisle seat pattern of boarding is best suited for individuals and business passengers.

I am sure we have all fell foul of this "Stupid Rule." A rule that is in place so that we can board business class or frequent flyer passengers first. It serves no other real purpose than to make people feel important.

It frustrates all other passengers, slows down boarding time, and causes flight delays.

It is great to see work to remove this stupid rule finally happen.

It can be challenging to ask the question that helps find the stupid rule. Let me give one example of how I sometimes approach this;

Recently in one of our German locations, I was in the woodyard warehouse speaking with a forklift driver. After shaking his hand and introducing myself, I asked, if you had ten thousand euros to spend on any safety improvement, what would you do?

The forklift driver replied they would install a barrier, gate, and improved safety signage in multiple languages. This measure would stop lorry drivers walking into a dangerous area unannounced and unsupervised.

Although this was already a rule in the warehouse, it was difficult to enforce and often ignored. Lorry drivers were in a hurry and didn't always speak the local language.

Maybe this is not a "Stupid Rule." However, it is undoubtedly an important rule that is not working. In my quest for eliminating "Stupid Rules," I uncovered this, and we were able to implement this great idea very quickly.

So, do not limit your search for stupid rules to safety. I can assure you that these exist in all areas of your business.

If you replace stupid rules with a safer way of working, you will keep people safe. You will also build your credibility and standing in your organisation.

QUESTION:

List three stupid rules that you know, and what could replace these?

A simple task for you to carry out:

Talk to the people doing the High-Risk jobs and find the stupid rules.

1. They know them.
2. They have the answer to working more safely.

THE STANDARD YOU WALK PAST IS THE STANDARD YOU ACCEPT

Be in no doubt how you behave as a leader, and the example you set will define and shape your future:

- Be visible.
- Take action when needed.
- Show commitment.

What I would like to do in this chapter is expand on how you can put this into practice, and get your leadership teams engaged.

A good friend of mine and an excellent role model, a Major in the Royal Army Medical Corps (RAMC), called me up and recommended I watch a video on YouTube. It has nothing to do with safety, rather bullying and transgender issues.

Lt General David Lindsay Morrison delivered it to the Australian Army.

I found it very moving; it has really profoundly influenced my behaviours and thinking.

This video and motivating talk are where I first heard the term:

"The standard you walk past is the standard you accept" ~ Lt General David Lindsay Morrison

I would highly recommend you watch the video.

If you want to change the culture in your organisation, then you have to develop your own and your leaders:

- Leadership & Communication skills.
- Training.
- Mentoring and coaching.
- Support.

So that they never walk past when someone is working unsafely, or they see an unsafe condition.

Let me give an example:

- The General Manager (GM) has decided that in his or her location, they are going to run a safety improvement program, and this will last approximately three years.

- As a result, all leaders will now participate in Safety walks, discussions, and observations.

- Two weeks ago, the GM walked your department, where you are the shift leader. The GM observed an operator using a box cutter knife and not wearing safety gloves.

- The safety rule clearly states when carrying out these tasks, operators must wear safety gloves. They have received training.

- After the violation was spotted, a safety discussion took place between the GM and the operator. Both the GM and operator agreed that safety gloves would be worn in the future while carrying out this task.

- As a result of the discussion and verbal agreement, no further action taken this time.

- However, today, you see the same person doing the same task without safety gloves. The operator sees you and quickly puts the safety gloves on.

Remember, the standard you walk past is the standard you accept:

1. If at this point, you do nothing, then this is the safety standard for this task in your department.
2. The breaking of safety rules is what you are personally willing to accept.
3. You, as the First Line Leader, have the most influence on this person by your action or inaction. It is not the General Manager, who is not involved in the day to day workings of this situation or location.

I have personally adopted this motto. I refer to it often and talk about it whenever I can. It clearly shows me the importance of challenging unsafe acts and conditions whenever we see them. It sets the standard of expectations and commitment in your organisation.

JEANETTE:

What I admire most about Stephen is his caring nature, and he won't walk on by when he sees a problem.

We both try to do one good deed a day. I have to say we don't always succeed! Our rules are no fuss, no looking for thanks if you see it fix it!

I will share two recent examples to show you what I mean:

1. The other day we were out walking our two German Shepherd dogs as we were walking along the main road we came across a raised utility hole cover that could have caused a severe injury to any cyclist that didn't see this hazard.

   At the time, Stephen was unable to replace it into a safe position — it was well and truly stuck.

   As we walked home together, we came across a building site where we asked if we could borrow a safety cone. We then walked the five hundred meters back with the cone and made the area as safe as possible. Once we got home, the problem was reported to the Local Highway Department for a permanent fix.

2. Stephen's dad told me a story that happened two weeks ago. They were driving home from playing golf together when they came across a person (volunteering) who was clearing rubbish from the grass verges, very close to the edge of the road. She was difficult to see, and the light was fading—so although she was doing a really worthwhile task, she was in danger.

   Stephen was able to pull into a layby approximately five hundred meters from this person. He then ran back and gave the volunteer one of the Hi-Visibility jackets that he keeps in the boot of his car so that she would be visible and safe by the road edge.

I know Stephen got a massive buzz when the person thanked him and put the hi-visibility jacket on, and she promised to wear it in the future.

That's what I think he means when he says the standard you walk past is the standard you accept.

It's more often than not just a small act, showing you care for the people you work and interact with.

QUESTION:

What stops people from taking immediate action in your organisation?

How can we help them overcome these barriers in the future?

What stops you from taking immediate action in your organisation?

How can you help yourself to overcome these barriers in the future?

COMMUNICATION

You are going to communicate the vision and plan through inspiring stories that create real meaning for people.

You are going to communicate and speak in a language that people can understand.

You are going to focus on implementation and getting the job done.

You are not going to bore or put people to sleep!

Let me share two great mnemonics from my days in the Military. These are so relevant to achieving good quality communications, and I will refer to them again in the Job Interviews Chapter of this book.

1. Prior Planning and Preparation Prevents Poor Performance (6 Ps).
2. Seldom is Time Wasted in Preparation (SITWIP).

Many years ago, I set my personal communication plan—I have shared this regularly with my teams ever since:

Stephen McNamara Communication Action Plan:

- Be visible.
- Be contactable.

- Speak face to face.
- Be approachable.
- Give feedback when asked a question & say thank you.

Some great communication tips I have learned from my German and Polish communication expert colleagues. They taught me you must have a reason and a purpose for communicating, don't do it only for communication's sake.

Thank you, Martin, Ingrid, Karo, Klaus, and Anna, you set the benchmark in a global organisation when we speak about communications:

- Less is more.
- Make it personal; speak from the heart - Use examples that mean something to you/ and them.
- Be authentic and genuine.
- Make it exciting and adapt your presentation or communication to your audience for maximum impact.
- Repeat your message (Vison & Plan).
- Check their understanding and get agreement.
- Know your subject, and don't bullshit.

If you are serious about becoming a success, then reduce your emails and text messages and get out and talk to people. Therefore, spend less time in your office hiding behind your computer screen and more time in face to face communication.

Keep all your presentations

- Simple.
- On-point.
- Exciting and as short on time as possible.

I work very hard to make sure every meeting I organise or run starts and finishes on time. Remember how frustrating it is to be in a meeting thirty minutes after it should have finished!

Not everyone is a natural communicator, and the thought of standing up and talking in front of a group of people can be nerve-racking to many.

You have to practice, practice, and practice, and one day, it might become natural or second nature for you.

I have known many successful people gain promotion purely because of their leadership and communication skills. You cannot neglect to develop these areas; they are crucial skills to have that will help you realise your vision and future potential.

JEANETTE:

I often hear people commenting on what a good communicator Stephen is at work. Then having him distant when you are talking to him at home can be frustrating. I know he is not listening, and his mind is on work.

I know he wouldn't read an email or interrupt an important conversation at work to take a phone call, so why is this acceptable at home?

The high level of success he has achieved has sometimes had a negative impact on his behaviours in his home life. He is not alone in this type of behavior as I see this in many other people too—*maybe this is you also?*

He turned him from being funny and enjoyable to be around. Instead, success brought a more serious, focussed person in his place

— someone who struggles to lose that more severe work persona in their home life.

I have seen too many relationships fail as a result of double standards. Communicate equally as well at home as you do at work.

On a positive note, over the last five years, we have done some simple things to bring the fun, enjoyment, and communication back into our life. One example I would like to share; We have purchased a motorhome, and we try and get away most weekends—when the weather permits, and sometimes when it doesn't.

In our motorhome, we have no TV and emails, and mobile phones are silent or switched off, sometimes we don't get a signal, which is even better, so no temptation!

As a result, we talk, walk our dogs, communicate, and have fun like we used to do. This small change has shown me we still have a great future together.

The advice I would give you is; work hard but do not lose the fun, keep talking, and sometimes slow down and enjoy the journey.

QUESTION:

What are your communication Strengths?

What are your communication weaknesses?

In priority order, what do you need to develop?

Who are excellent communicators in your life, and why do you rate them so highly?

FOCUS ON PEOPLE AT THE FRONT OF THE TRAIN

You are going on a journey you have the vision, plan, and you have shared within your teams the direction of travel.

You have to make the journey personal, engaging, and motivating to your teams, they need to have a stake in its outcome.

They are valued members of the team – *it most often than not will not work without them!*

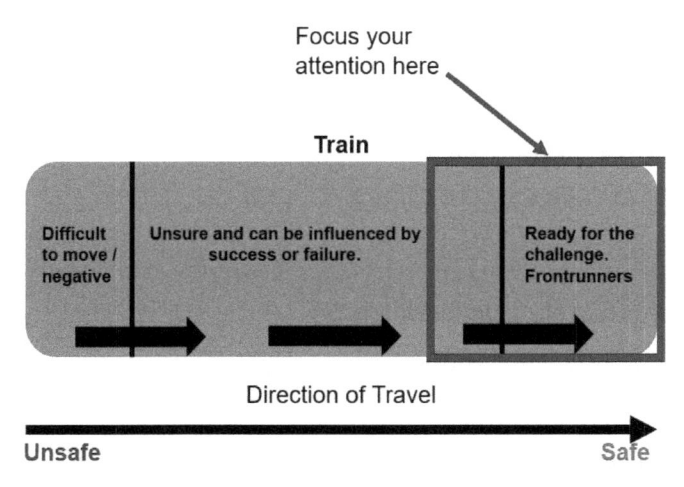

Train

Focus your attention here

| Difficult to move / negative | Unsure and can be influenced by success or failure. | Ready for the challenge. Frontrunners |

Direction of Travel

Unsafe — Safe

©2019 Copyright Stephen McNamara

Be a Success

#NO REVERSE GEARS ON THIS TRAIN!

In my experience, it is very easy for your plans to be derailed and brought to a standstill by negativity, inactivity, or problematic behaviour.

Therefore, we are going to focus all our efforts on the front of the train, where our leaders and ambassadors reside.

We can spend a disproportionate amount of time trying to appease the most disruptive or difficult (back of the train) people in the organisation. This time is better spent working on the people who want to take part and see success.

You can spend 100 percent of your time with 10 percent of the people, and no matter how hard you try, you will never change their opinion. It can also take time away from the very people who are going to help you drive your vision and plan forward. Therefore, we are going to focus on our positive people and not worry about the negative.

Beware of the disruptive or destructive:

- We don't do it like that.
- That will never work.
- What do you know.
- I won't do that.

I can guarantee you the person who one day replaces me in my current job will be from the front of the train!

So let us start rewarding:

- Good behaviours & values.
- Positivity.

- Good ideas and best practices.
- Good quality work.
- People who care for each other.
- The person prepared to go the extra mile.

We are going to make it exciting, fun, worthwhile, and rewarding to be at the front of the train, i.e., leading this journey. If you want to have opportunity, development and highlight your potential, then it is clear for all to see on the train the best seats are at the front.

The people in the middle of the train have not yet entirely made their minds up. They are looking to see which direction the train is going. So let us make all these people want to come to the front too.

We never reward unwanted (back of the train) behaviors;

- No time & effort.
- No distraction.
- No credibility.
- No focus.
- No change of plan.
- No value.

Anyone at the back of the train will have a choice move forward (come on board) or get off. It is the easiest thing in the world to highlight problems, challenge ideas, or improvements.

However, if a person at the back of the train is really looking to move forward, what a great chance this is for you to step forward and help.

An excellent recent real-life example of 'front of the train thinking' I would like to share:

Background:

- A part of an organisation has a problem with Heavy Goods Vehicles (HGV) arriving overloaded.
- The maximum legal weight is 40 tons, and sometimes the HGV's can weigh 55 tons = 38% overweight.
- They have tried many times to get their suppliers complying with the law. However, this has proven difficult to sustain.

Solution

- Today a fine is levied against the haulier if any HGV is found to be overweight.
- The penalties are all collected and retained.
- At the end of the year, all the haulage companies that sent deliveries on or below 40 tons get paid an equal share of the fines received from the companies that failed to comply.
- The good companies must use their share of the penalty for driver safety training.

What a great example of rewarding good behaviour and not focussing time and effort chasing unwanted behaviour.

There is an excellent quote from one of the most celebrated authors that would be perfect to close this chapter:

> *Never argue with stupid people. They'll drag you down to their level and beat you with experience – Mark Twain*

To summarise:

1. *Focus on the positive and not worry about the negative.*
2. *Help people who have a genuine desire to change.*
3. *Reward good behaviour.*
4. *Do not reward unwanted behaviour.*

YOU GET OUT WHAT YOU PUT IN

The great news is your success is within your own hands and destiny. How much you want it and how hard you are prepared to work to get it is really up to you—*Therefore, you're going to work smart (not waste your energy) and follow your plan.*

Today everything seems to be about speed, and the average attention span is getting close to zero. However, let us be very clear there are no shortcuts to success, and I can promise you it will not fall onto your lap—No one is going to walk up to you and just give you the success you want.

So you are going to try and make success happen and take opportunities when they arise; you and I both know that they don't come around very often. So, don't expect more until you are prepared to do more. If you are going to be successful, then you are going to have to work hard. You have to *"walk the talk."*

One example I would like to share to help you understand my point: My favourite sport is tennis I play hard, I play to win, and I am deeply competitive. One of my strengths on the court is I chase and fight for every point. I always try and work harder than my opponent! That said I want to play fairly, I want to enjoy the game and I know that sometimes I will lose.

When I lose, it's not the end of the world, and I always congratulate the person who was good enough to beat me. I often go away to think about and practice what I could do to win the next time we play.

When I think of my journey, I worked hard for many years to build a credible education, and I took some opportunities that other people passed. As we have already and will further discuss, you will need to sort out your emotional leadership skills and a base level of education. You are not going to wait for someone to do this for you. Otherwise, You may be waiting for a very long time! That said, I am a great believer that sometimes you also make your own luck. Let me share a story of a long-standing work friend who has done exceptionally well:

> I remember this person years ago covering a role for a senior colleague who was going to be off work for many months.
>
> At this point in their life, they were a machine operator on shift work, definitely thinking about how to improve their promotion prospects.
>
> He/she was not the first choice for the job role someone else better qualified and more highly thought of got the opportunity first.
>
> That said, for whatever reason, it did not work out for the first choice person. As a result, the company asked if my work friend could now cover this role;
>
> *They took a pay cut, and they worked longer hours, they increased their workload.*

On the positive side, they gained exposure to the management team for twelve months, built their credibility, and people knew their name for the right reasons. So all the hard work, heartache, and increases in workload meant they gained promotion to a manager position soon after this secondment finished. Today they are a very senior well-respected person within my company. *Sometimes in business, you have to take a step backward to move forward.*

WORKLIFE BALANCE

Many great business legends have spoken about working twice as hard as your rivals or competition; for example, *"If you work 80 hours a week, then you will accomplish things 2 times faster than someone who works 40 hours a week."* — Elon Musk

Let us be absolutely clear these types of people are truly exceptional and one in a million! However, that does not mean you cannot be successful in your own right and do it your way.

I have always thought that you must strive to maintain the right work-life balance for your mental health and physical wellbeing. You can not perform to your full potential if you are unwell or not functioning at 100 percent.

I think it is essential when thinking about the success that you desire that you manage work-life to achieve the quality of the home-life you want.

Sometimes it is difficult to have both!

I remember a time in my life, not so long ago when I simultaneously held three jobs at the same time:

1. Production Manager in a global company.
2. Owner/ Director of a Ltd Company providing training.
3. Football Safety Officer working weekends.

I was earning great money, and my Ltd company was going from strength to strength. I employed six part-time trainers, and this business was booming.

However, no matter how much money I was making, it wasn't sustainable in the long term, not if I wanted to be a good father and husband, or I could chase the money and lose what I valued most.

Many successful people I know today are divorced or have relationships both at work and home that are at crisis point.

You don't want to be this person!

On this journey, you have undertaken you to have to try to strike the right balance. If you can get this support network right, then this is one less thing to cause you to worry.

I would not have had opportunities and promotions without the support of my wife and family. However, I haven't always got it right. It really can be a juggling act of multiple priorities, and you are trying to keep all the balls in the air.

Therefore some simple rules I try (not always successfully) to follow:

- Finish work on time whenever I can.
- Make sure my team finishes on time.
- Don't travel unnecessarily on the weekends.
- No work emails or phone calls when I am on holiday.

- Talk to my boss at the earliest opportunity if I have a personal family issue that might impact on my work.
- Listen to my family if my work is impacting on our home life.
- Talk to my family at the earliest opportunity if I know my workload is increasing, so they are aware of the short term impacts.
- Don't always prioritise work over family commitments whenever there is a conflict.

A good friend of mine once told me: *"work is work; it lasts eight hours, and when it is over, it is over!"* —She was so disciplined and was able to switch off the moment she went home. Jeanette can testify because of my love of the work I do today. I still struggle with mixing work and home life commitments.

The higher up the promotion ladder you go it can feel the higher the expectation on you regarding commitment, travel, and workload.

So this is a topic that you need to be mindful of; otherwise, you might end up sleepwalking into a situation that can cause divorce, separation, high anxiety, and stress.

JEANETTE:

Money is lovely, but sometimes it becomes the focus of people's lives. What you should remember is money isn't everything and how much do you need to be happy?

Work out what is most important to you in your life and don't ignore or neglect it!

When Stephen is flying around the world, and I am left at home alone, I sometimes wonder if all these trips are really needed. Does he feel he needs to be there instead of him *having* to be there? I remember many years ago Stephen phoning me from Italy and saying what a fantastic view he had from his hotel, and what a great place it was. At the time, I was trying to bath two screaming children. We agreed that I didn't need to know how great the location, food, or wine was in the future.

My advice is to be mindful and respectful of your support network and family. Don't overlook or forget us as we are an essential part of your success story.

JOB INTERVIEWS

When writing this chapter, it really got me thinking about the number and type of job interviews I have attended over thirty-eight years of continuous employment.

I have attended three job interviews in the last five years and been fortunate that I was successful in all three of them—I say this not to boast or show off. Instead, I want to show you that, for some reason, I have a simple recipe for success that works when it comes to job interviews and carer advancement. Let's discuss this further:

I always treat internal and external job interviews the same.

Let me recap two great sayings I learned in the Army and still use today when thinking about job interviews;

- *Prior Planning and Preparation Prevents Poor performance (6 Ps).*
- *Seldom is Time Wasted in Preparation (SITWIP).*

For the job interview itself, always understand the basics, i.e., knowledge of the company, job role, expected dress code, language, and timings.

If I am ever unsure whether to wear a suit, In that situation I would always wear a suit.

I am always positive about the new challenge and job role.

It is okay to be nervous, and it shows how much you actually want the job and that you care deeply. However, don't let your nerves overwhelm you.

On these occasions, "put your big boy/ girl pants on" look them in the eye, shake their hands, and tell your story. I am sure your life story and experiences is an interesting one to tell.

Look at your vision and cross-reference with your plan. Is this position right for you? Does it match your personality, skill sets, and motivation? If not, can you develop these weaknesses so you are not so exposed, and ultimately, you can be successful If the answer is no, then I would not apply

Don't become a serial job applier; it can sometimes make you look desperate.

Understand the context of the organisation, location, or department. What challenges are they facing and what are the key skills they are wanting.

For Example: if I was applying for a Sales Directors' vacancy. I would think hard about; Is it communication, leadership, and softer skills they are seeking and Is having a technical ability secondary in this instance.

Once you understand this, you can then think about what is your Unique Selling Point. What differentiates you from the other candidates and aim to build on this during the interview discussions.

Listen carefully and let the interviewer ask the question entirely. We can all have the temptation to butt in or speak over someone, often made worse by nerves.

If you didn't understand the question the first time around, be brave and ask for it to be repeated.

I have never attended any job interview (internally or externally) with stacks of graphs or performance figures loaded onto a PowerPoint presentation. The people who are interviewing you know this information already, or if they don't, they should.

More recently, I have used my vision and plan as a basis for the interview discussion.

When you sell yourself, be honest. Always give credit to the teams you have enjoyed success with. Without a doubt, it will be because of these teams that you are sat in the room today, hoping to gain that long-awaited promotion or a new career opportunity. Just think how good it is to be able to show you are a natural leader, one that encourages teams to develop and flourish.

Understand what your weaknesses are concerning the job vacancy. If questioned, be brave, acknowledge these.

Everyone has flaws, and no one person is the complete package. Give good positive examples of how you are trying to improve in your weak areas and focus on your strengths.

At the end of the interview no matter how well you thought it went always look your interviewers in the eye, shake hands, and say thank you

Practice your interviews with someone you trust, get them to ask the hard questions, and let them give honest, constructive feedback.

Don't worry! Most people walk out and spend the next few hours or days analysing how the interview went. It is only natural, and we all do it!

JEANETTE:

I would always take an opportunity to get feedback on why I wasn't successful.

I always remember a close family friend who was unsuccessful in a high-level job interview.

Although at the time she was unsuccessful, she actively sought feedback from the interview panel to improve her chances in future job interviews. Unbeknown to her, she was the only unsuccessful candidate to go and request this type of feedback.

The employer was so impressed that she took this proactive approach that they offered her an alternative job, which she accepted.

I think this is an excellent example of having a positive mindset and never giving up when things didn't go your way.

Never give up if it's a job you want then apply again in the future. You might have to give it more than one attempt before you are successful.

MEASURE IMPROVEMENT AND SUCCESS

Be disciplined and focussed—do not try to measure everything.

Understand what needs measuring and why and stick rigorously to these, anything else can cause a distraction or interfere with reaching your targets – keep your focus and eyes on the goal.

Do not overload your meetings with slide after slide of safety, production, or quality measures I can guarantee it will be a slow and painful experience for all involved.

This approach turns people away and can be monotonous and boring. It has quite the opposite effect of the one you wanted to achieve.

How many meetings have you attended when it has been challenging to stay awake – quite literally, it can be death by PowerPoint. *Do not let that be one of your meetings!*

JEANETTE:

Why not ask your family how could you measure your success and achievement and find out what is important to them.

So don't limit this to work activities, why not measure:

- The time you spend with your loved ones.
- The quality of the activities you do at home.
- How many times you laugh and smile.
- What did you used to do that you don't do today.

QUESTION:

What do you measure today that you would keep?

What current measures add no value to your organisation, and why is this?

How are you going to make the change from traditional measures to ones that add real value?

What are the pitfalls if you take this approach?

EVOLUTION V REVOLUTION

● ● ● ● ● ● ● ● ● ● ● ●

When taking on a new job role, responsibility, or project, you must think about the impact you want to make, the scale and scope of the task ahead.

Your vision and plan influence this critical decision, as well as what you know of the companies, priorities, people, culture, and finances.

I might show it this way:

Level of Ambition – Where do YOU want to be ?

1. Management Commitment and Visibility
2. Leaders taking responsibility
3. Behavioural safety
4. Rigorously identify all high risk activities and make safe

Safety Standards

2020 Safety

2012 Safety

The greater pressure is always downwards i.e. to do less not more!

Best Practice

Safe

Unsafe

Dangerous

©2019 Copyright Stephen McNamara

So is it evolution or revolution?

Definition: The two nouns evolution and revolution both refer to a change. However, there is a distinctive difference between the change implied by these two words.

Evolution:

Refers to a slow and gradual change. This change is small steps over a defined period of time to reach your goal. It could be about taking a step back and looking at the work that has already been completed. Ensuring nothing was missed and the quality was good enough the first time around. It could also involve introducing new thoughts and ideas. In this context, it is not always a large company program; it is about evolving and nurturing improvements.

Revolution:

Whereas revolution refers to a sudden, dramatic, and complete transformation. It could be a fundamental change in both root and branch, i.e., a step-change in safety, quality, or a productivity program. It is an opportunity to influence the whole organisation in its way of behaving and thinking. It is a radical far-reaching program that has a long-lasting impact on every employee affected. By its very nature, it may take significant time (maybe years) before you can say you have completed the program.

For example, I have recently taken on a new job role within an established part of the business. It was apparent much work over several years has already been done with a limited degree of success. *In this instance, for me, Evolution, not Revolution, was the priority.*

QUESTION:

What do you think is needed in your organisation, department, or job role for you to reach your vision?

1. Is it evolution – Why is that?

2. Or is it revolution – Why is that?

SPEED/NUMBERS V QUALITY

The balance you have to strike when taking on any new challenge can be how fast to implement, and the quality of the change or outcome you want to see.

I am sure we are all great at starting new programs, projects, or initiatives. What I often see is we are not so great at successfully closing or completing them.

You have to understand what you are trying to achieve and what is the organisations current capacity. Realistically how long will it take to implement? Your focus is on the quality needed to make the change successful and sustained.

You have to try to get a good understanding of:

- What is the current situation within the organisation?
- What is the priority right now?
- What is there ambition level?
- What might hold you back?
- What could drive you forward?
- Where are the high risks?

You cannot overburden the organisation to the extent that it is overwhelmed. That said, if you do nothing, then nothing changes.

Therefore, you are going to choose your battles carefully.

It is sometimes a delicate balance with conflicting priorities. People will be more comfortable to come on board if they understand the scale, speed, and quality of work required.

Trust me; no one wants to work any more than needed. Most people are busy and have a full workload already. Therefore, Keep focused.

You set SMART objectives:

- Specific.
- Measurable.
- Achievable.
- Realistic.
- Targeted.

If there is an immediate safety, quality, cost production issue, then a faster speed of change or implementation, maybe the only course of action.

The quality may have to come later!

For example; I have seen in many companies where they have started OHS programs for safety walks, observations, and discussions. The main focus in the early period is getting the numbers, i.e., getting the program started or moving, i.e., building good traction.

What can often happen is no real check on the quality or participation percentage of the workforce.

So you might have 60 percent of the workforce doing all the safety walks and 40 percent not engaged and not likely to be involved because the overall numbers are on target.

Because the numbers are looking good, there might not be a real focus on the quality! It can be a vicious circle often challenging to break. The critical issue in the example I have used above is the Quality, not necessarily the speed or numbers.

So maybe the answer in this instance is to reduce the number of walks required per person and not incentivise this measure. I would always much rather, incentivise the quality of the work done and participation percentage of the workforce rather than an arbitrary number.

The recent COVID 19 Pandemic has also highlighted what I mean by speed/ numbers v quality. Let me use this as another example:

There was a well documented global shortage of Personal Protective Equipment (PPE) for our hospitals, frontline medics, and careworkers. This shortage has meant organisations having to switch from the quality of the product to speed and numbers. So they have to use inferior or reduced quality items because these items are more readily available and can be manufactured and sourced quicker.

The reality of the situation is people will be at more risk. However, it has been decided at Governmental/ National levels that a lesser level of PPE protection is better than no protection.

The different health organisations are then having to revise their safety procedures to accommodate this massive change to try and keep medics, careers, and patients safe.

In an ideal world, it would always be the best quality PPE first.

Some points to further consider:

- It is not always a black and white choice of Speed / Numbers over Quality. Most times, you are trying to do both. However, one (Speed or Quality) often has a slightly higher priority than the other due to the circumstances on the ground.

- If you decide speed or numbers is the key driver, at some point, I can guarantee you that you will have to come back and refocus on the quality—think of the COVID 19 Pandemic example I used above. *Therefore, you should understand that only prioritising speed or numbers is not sustainable in the long term.*

- The larger the scope or challenge, i.e., company-wide, then the more difficult it is to transfer the knowledge and skills successfully.

- You have to be realistic in your timelines and speed of implementation.

- Don't over promise and under deliver.

QUESTION:

To be successful, what actions/tasks do you need to carry out:

Is speed the priority – why is this?

Is quality the priority – why is this?

HOW TO DEAL WITH SETBACKS

Why do we fall? So that we can learn to pick ourselves up ~ Michael Caine, Batman Begins 2005.

Remember: all humans fail.

I am a great believer that "things" happen for a reason, and how you deal with a setback or failure is more important and shows more about your real character than how you deal with success.

Why do I think this? Everybody can show a smiley face or be happy when things are going right. I have seen many good people not realise their full potential because they can not get over a setback or failure.

I am sure we have all seen people apply for jobs who are unsuccessful. Who then go on to sulk or bad mouth the successful candidate.

You are not this person.

Every day is a job interview ~ Unknown.

You are going to keep positive because you have a clear vision and a plan, and you understand if you work hard with focus one day, your time will come.

Don't rush to apportion blame on others; you may never know when your next opportunity will arrive; it could even be tomorrow.

I remember a conversation with an employee (let's call her Sam) Sam had applied for a more senior managers position. Her current employment was as a sales coordinator, about two levels below the vacant position.

On the day in question, we met by the office coffee machine, and I could see she was upset and a little downhearted. Although I recognised Sam and I knew her name, we did not really know each other, other than in passing and small talk.

I clearly recall our discussion on that day. My advice to her was to be brave, and at the earliest opportunity to wish the successful candidate good luck in their new position, no matter how raw or difficult, this might be for her to do. To go back to work with a positive outlook and try to get over her disappointment as quickly as possible.

We had a good fifteen minutes trying to turn this negative to a positive.

Even today, I often think about that brief conversation. Several months later, I was pleased to hear that Sam had been successful, and she had gained a well-deserved promotion. I am not sure what effect my talk had on her. However, I could see a person who needed support, a kind word, and some practical advice.

Remember a kind word costs nothing.

I bumped into Sam while writing this book, and we both remembered the talk that day. She has kindly agreed to put her thoughts down on paper on how she remembered our discussion and what she did as a result:

In Sams own words:

What I remember most was; you were saying something along the lines of: 'it's what you do next and how you handle this that matters most now,' as well as 'remember to congratulate the successful candidate.'

Q. Did it help me, and why was that? Yes absolutely! I wasn't going to let my disappointment define me. I decided to view it as an extension to the interview - I would continue to be a professional no matter how down or hurt I was currently feeling.

Q. What did I do as a result? I actively sought feedback and worked on areas I could develop.

Q. Have I ever done something similar as a result? Yes, I have had the opportunity to use your words with others who find themselves in the same position and often refer to our 'kitchen chat.'

I am so pleased to find out that Sam found our conversation helpful in her time of need. It just shows you how powerful fifteen minutes of quality time can be. We will both remember that conversation for a very long time.

Like I have said, you just never know when the next opportunity is coming. You are going to:

1. Work hard to be cheerful and positive all the time.
2. Put things into perspective.
3. Not sulk, be bitter, badmouth, or get angry when you don't get what you want.
4. Take the rough with the smooth no one said life was going to be easy.

Never give up on your dream:

Let me wrap up this chapter by talking about my eldest son. From the age of eight to fourteen, he was an average ability club swimmer, and he would attend swim training four times a week.

Most of the time, when it came to competitions, he would finish just outside the medal placings. However, he never badmouthed anyone. He was proud to be part of the team. We, as parents, we're very proud of his attitude and good "sportsman" nature—he was and remains a great team player.

At fourteen years old, he was dropped from the swim team and was hurt by this decision, although he put a brave face on it.

The same few people were always the winners, and as a result, they were given most of the chances and opportunities when it came to competitions. That said, they had never experienced losing, and when they moved up to a higher level, many could not cope with that experience and emotion—Winning for many of them was everything. Nothing else mattered!

Gary persevered on his own. He never gave up. Today he is a top-class triathlete, and in 2017 broke the Guinness World Record for the Fastest Marathon Time Dressed as A Fast Food Item—a record he still holds today. The losses and disappointments he had experienced as a child that he fought hard to overcome subsequently have made the successes that he now enjoys today that much sweeter.

We are so proud that he never gave up.

So my question to you is: why can't this be you?

TAKE A RISK

If you or your team can bring good ideas that add value to your business or organization, It will help build your credibility, profile, and generate positivity – Always r*emember, no stupid rules!*

You do not bring stupid rules or ideas to your organisation.

Don't let the thought or worry of failure, stop your plans and innervation; if you don't take a risk or try new ideas, then nothing really changes.

Writing this book is an example of what I mean. I am not sure what you, the reader, will think of the book. You may view it as a load of nonsense or of no use to you.

That said, this book has been in my head as an idea for some time. In my opinion, we don't do enough today to help our people with future potential to navigate their way to success.

I sincerely hope my book can help with this. However, as you can see, it is a significant personal and financial risk to me. If you want to succeed and get on in life, then you have to sometimes back yourself and step out of your comfort zone—if you do nothing, you get nothing.

All the people I know who are successful have taken a risk and not played it safe at some point in their career. That said, they are not serial risk takers either.

You are going to choose your risk opportunities carefully and cross-reference with your vision and plan.

My youngest son and I play a lot of tennis, and I remember my son's professional tennis coach drilling him on how to win matches.

During these training exercises every time my son received a ball back from his coach, he had to shout out loudly one of the three following options based on how he was going to play his next shot:

1. Defend
2. Neutral
3. *Attack =, i.e., taking a risk*

It was fascinating to watch this, in his early days of coaching, 40 percent of my sons' groundstrokes were either defensive or neutral, with 60 percent attacking.

Meaning when he was in a rally, he saw every other ball as a winning opportunity—He was a serial risk-taker and, as a consequence, lost most of his tennis matches in the early part of his career.

You cannot win in tennis or business with this approach; in reality, you only have a small percentage of real clear cut opportunities to really attack the ball or take a risk.

As already said, you are not going to be a serial risk-taker rather. You are someone who recognises that most weeks and months, you are working in defensive or neutral mode, i.e., doing your day to day work in a positive mindset to your best ability with no fuss or dramas.

However, you are ready for when you come across a great idea, and you are brave enough to take a risk and bring this great idea forward.

One recent example I would like to share with you:

I attended a Safety Summit, and the guest speaker challenged us to "think about safety differently."

Asking the question; How can we measure safety in the now!

After a short group discussion, one idea that our team came away with as a result of being asked this was:

Why not use a device that you see in toilets/washrooms all over the world:

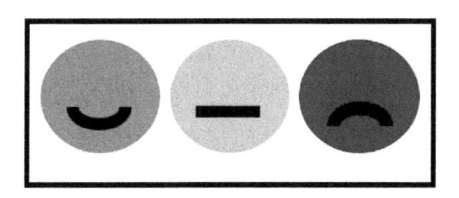

©2019 Copyright Stephen McNamara

And why not ask the question:

>How safe was your day?
>Or
>Did you work safely today?

There is a risk in using this type of device, and there are many risks if you think about it.

Can you imagine the benefits If you can get this working correctly?

These benefits include being able to measure safety, including people's feelings and perspectives in real-time—*However, that said, it is a risk!*

I have another example that is personal to me that I would like to share with you when thinking about taking a risk; I once attended a three-day training course where there were twenty delegates, each paying £500—the training provider was generating £10,000.

In mine and some of the other delegate's opinions, the course tutor was not very good, and I walked away very underwhelmed and uninspired. Unfortunately, for me, my key takeaway from that three-day session was I could have done a much better job myself.

So I took a risk; I set up my own Ltd training company (while in full-time employment with permission from my employer). I employed four high-quality trainers, and I set myself the personal challenge of making £2500 profit per training session. I have to say I didn't quite manage to achieve this goal. However, I was not too far away either.

I could have sat back moaned about the quality of the training and simply done nothing about it. Instead, I took a personal risk, and I set up my own successful training company, which I sold for a good profit several years later.

So don't be afraid to take a risk; after all, you are trying to turn your dreams into reality.

JEANETTE:

I remember when Stephen left the army at that time, we had recently married, purchased our first house, and I was pregnant with twins. He came home one day and just presented this major bombshell on my lap—it was a done deal, no turning back.

As a result, I spent many weeks worrying about how we would live, pay our mortgage, and feed our new family when it arrived. He made this hugely important decision by himself with no discussion or consultation between us—it was a massive risk.

If we had discussed this at the time together, I am sure we would have come to the same conclusion. However, I definitely felt like I was on the outside looking inwards.

Today when we have risky decisions to make, it is a team effort. It's done together and not in isolation.

When Stephen was recently discussing his thoughts for this book, the time, effort, pitfalls, personal and financial risks—it was a joint decision to go ahead full steam.

So my advice to you is when you are making an important decision about taking a risk is to involve your loved ones or people you trust:

> *We will give good advice,*
> *We will be good sounding boards*
> *We don't want you to fail we want you to succeed,*
> *We want to be part of your journey and help, however, and whenever we can.*

Don't sideline us as we are part of your team

QUESTION:

When did you last take a risk?

Why did taking the risk work, or why did it backfire?

With hindsight, what would you do differently?

What are the barriers to you taking a risk?

What are the enablers to you taking a risk?

EDUCATION AND TRAINING

Early in my career, my lack of education wasn't necessarily an issue or barrier to me, gaining promotions, and increasing my salary. However, as I started to progress, it was clear that I needed to build and give this extra attention. *I have always thought I had emotional leadership skills. However, would this be enough for me to get where I ultimately wanted to get too —longer-term probably not!*

I want you to think of yourself as an empty toolbox, and you are going to fill this with the right tools for the job. I think one thing that I have seen in people that have ultimately gone on to succeed is they have actively thought about:

1. What would my company support and fund?
2. What to do in my own time using my funding?
3. What did I need to learn to do my job well or to progress further?

They have taken it upon themselves to develop and improve their education and training in their own time:

- It helped them build the needed knowledge and experience.
- Showed the company that they had the drive and commitment to do this development outside of working hours, and incurring cost to themselves.
- They were more committed to attend and learn on the course as they paid for it.

Therefore, you are taking responsibility for your own education and training, and you are not leaving this solely in the company's hands.

Once you start your training and development, you will find it helps you open doors that you might otherwise think impossible.

For example:

- I remember interviewing an employee who had started an in-house training course that would last one year (NVQ Level 3 in Continuous Production Management).

- Ten people started the course, and after seven months for various reasons, only two people completed the training and evaluation.

- It was just great for that person to show how much they had grown, learned new skills, and put the training into practice.

- It was an excellent opportunity for them to shine in a job interview environment. They demonstrated that they could stick to a difficult task and not quit if the going got tough.

Therefore, don't just do any training and development; they are a significant investment in your time and effort.

Be focussed:

- What areas do I need to develop personally?
- What are my strengths and weaknesses?
- Where does the company need development and support?
- Where are the company's strengths and weaknesses?
- Does the training support my vision and plan?

You must continually strive to grow as a person, develop your skills, and work on your weaknesses.

Over the last ten years, I have tried to build a solid foundation in:

1. OHS.
2. Communication skills.
3. Leadership.
4. Coaching and mentoring.

It is a journey that never ends; you will never be perfect (no one is); we all have flaws, strengths, and weaknesses.

JEANETTE:

Stephen, in his early days, did not have enough qualifications to progress to where he is now.

When he went on courses, it was often a long slow process. However, when he started his Diploma in Safety Qualification, he thought he could pass with not to much effort.

I remember when he did his first assignment; it took him less than one hour, and he was very confident that it would be marked as a good level pass mark.

I was working on my social care qualifications at the same time, and I was shocked that he could do his assignment so quickly. I thought he must really know his stuff!

When his course tutor called to say he had failed the assignment, I was secretly a little bit pleased as I had been working all hours to get my pass marks certainly much harder than he was working!

It was a good lesson he needed to learn if you want something then you are going to have to work hard to get it. Sometimes you will get a knockback, but you don't walk away. You come back and try again.

At the time he was ready to quit the course and walk away, it was only after me telling him to get a grip and stop being overdramatic that we were then able to sit down together and calmly plan his next steps.

So my message to you is; get that education you need, it won't be easy, don't quit when it gets tough, and it will really help you move forward in your career and aspirations when you eventually pass.

QUESTION:

What training or personal development have you done the past twelve months that will help you be successful?

What do you need to do in the next 12 months?

What is stopping you?

What support do you need, and where can you find this?

COACHING AND MENTORING

I have been very fortunate and had the pleasure of formally mentoring three work colleagues. It is a fantastic experience to see these people gain confidence, flourish, and realise their success.

I believe all three people gained promotion and success as a direct result of committing and engaging in a mentoring program. I am sure they would have been successful anyway. However, the mentoring program helped focus their minds and activities. I am convinced it was the reason they got there quicker.

Mentoring works both ways, and I felt I got just as much out of the experience as the mentee.

So I would highly encourage you to seek a mentor, a person you can build trust with, one who will listen, advise, challenge, coach, and inspire you.

This person will be encouraging and positive in their approach to coaching / mentoring.

So my challenge to you is to go out and find this person, and I can guarantee you will improve your chances of success if you do.

I have asked the first person I mentored to give some feedback on her mentoring experience. She has gone on to be very successful and highly respected. Here are Tracey's thoughts and ideas in her own words. I think it is great to get practical insight from someone who has actually been through one of these programmes.

TRACEY:

What makes a good mentor in your opinion?:

I would say that in our experience, the fact that you came from a different background really helped as you were able to put a different opinion/spin on the issues I was facing. You had a positive outlook and were very approachable. We set out the guidelines for the mentoring programme that fitted with us both, i.e., our values, our commitments, aims, and goals.

Why did it work for you?:

I was coming into a new and challenging role with no leadership experience. The team was pretty much broken, so there were going to be a lot of challenges. You gave me ideas on how to get some small wins straight away, which helped the team to grow their trust in my ability. When we tackled more complicated situations, you were unbiased, fair but, at the same time, pushed me out of my comfort zone with mutual agreement. We reflected on what went well and what we could improve. You helped me to create my own personal development plan and ensured through regular meetings that I was following the plan.

What did you get out of it?:

In the beginning, I was nervous and self-conscious about a lot of decisions and discussions I needed to have, but each time a challenge arose, you were there to help me plan and execute what needed to be done. I grew in confidence and resilience during our mentoring, and I looked forward to discussing things that went well. We also got to a point in the relationship where I would give you advice and challenge you.

Why did we (mentor and mentee) gel and it work so well?:

I think that it worked well as we were matched in our values, outlook on life, and had mutual respect for each other. We faced similar situations together and individually. We set out on a journey that was new to us both. I believe we thrived on that and proved with the correct mentor/mentee match; the programme works well.

Any other comments

The mentoring programme really worked well for me, and today I actively encourage my team members to go through a similar experience. It helped me focus my efforts on what was important. I'm flattered that you wanted to include me in this part of your life, and I wish you the very best for the future.

JEANETTE:

I do not doubt in my mind that I am Stephen's main coach and mentor. I would never let him fall or fail. I always tell him the truth, and he will often go away and reflect on my comments and guidance.

I know he greatly appreciates my openness and honesty even though we don't always see eye to eye. When we don't agree, it's quite funny to see Stephen will go away, think about what we have discussed, and, more often than not, come back and say sorry and agree with my original point of view.

He will often ask me for advice on how to deal with testing and demanding situations at work, and I know he trusts me to help whenever I can.

That said, you can see throughout the book we have had to have some difficult and challenging conversations, and this has put a strain on our relationship at times.

I can only encourage you to work on having this level of openness and trust in your partner; after all, it's a team effort.

QUESTION:

Would you consider engaging with a mentor or coach?

Who could do this role for you?

Why have you answered, Yes or No?

What is stopping you?

What benefits do you see?

Are there any organisations that might provide this service free of charge?

NEXT STEPS

As I move to the end of my carer and reflect on what I have accomplished, I can say with confidence that I have always strived to leave my workplace in better shape than I found it. Hopefully, the people I have worked with will develop some of my beliefs, thoughts, and ideas – The same ideas that I, in turn, role modeled from the inspiring people I have met and worked with over many years.

Try and enjoy your work; life is hard enough!

Okay, my part has finished; it is now over to you.

Some people are happy where they are and will stay within there comfort zone for the duration of their working life. Let me say I believe this is okay. However, I am guessing this is not you.

You will have to continually challenge yourself if you are going to succeed.

Your success is in your hands, in a nutshell:

- What's your vision?
- What's your plan?
- What are your most significant risks?
- Develop your emotional leadership skills.

- Work on your education.
- Build your team and trust.
- Work hard.
- Build your reputation and standing.
- Measure your success.
- Take a risk when the opportunity is right.

No one person has the answer for you. Take what you need from the book, mix it with other books or experiences, and come up with a formula that works for you—after all, it is your success.

You have to work at getting that formula right; no one is going to come and give you success. However, you can take control of your journey. I would welcome any comments and feedback, and I would love to hear if this book has helped you untap your potential.

I wish I had a book like this when I was muddling through I might have made fewer mistakes and arrived a little bit quicker than I did!

I will leave the very last part of this book with a thought-provoking observation from my wife. The other night she was watching a television program about a terminally ill young woman. Knowing that I was writing this book, she talked me through what she had just heard.

The reporter had asked the very ill young woman what her legacy was and what was her most significant achievement. She replied, without any hesitation, *"look at my two wonderful children."*

Don't think of your success in purely monetary terms; why limit yourself it can be anything and everything you want it to be!

JEANETTE:

A saying I often quote to Stephen that I would like to share with you all is, "it is nice to be important, but it is more important to be nice."

Be a kind person, always do the right thing, and I am a true believer that the rest will fall into place

Good luck

MENTAL HEALTH

We both thought we had reached the end of the book, but recent family events have moved us to write one more short chapter.

The world can be a shitty place sometimes and were all struggling in our own way to get through each day.

Today Mental Health still has a stigma attached to it that prevents people from seeking help and support. The smile you see on the outside can be masking a person in dire straights on the inside.

The journey to success isn't about breaking anybody—My sincere hope is that you are going to be a kind, caring person.

We recently saw a TV documentary program in a workplace where the manager was highlighting his skills as a good leader because 50 percent of new starter employees he emotionally destroyed within the first three months of employment. As a result, broken and bruised, they subsequently left the company.

In his opinion, the new employees that stayed would go on and be successful. They had survived his baptism of fire. They could now handle anything work would through up.

This dismal record was his badge of honour that he wore with pride! What a horrible piece of work he is, and I am sure one day he will get a taste of the medicine he freely dishes out to others—I am a firm believer in Karma.

Look after your family and the people you work with; if you think they are struggling to cope, then take time out to talk with them. Offer them a helping hand, show them care and consideration. If needed, get them to seek medical help and support. Don't walk on by—be brave and help.

If you are the one who is suffering, then please go and seek help, so you're able to learn how to cope with the lows and enjoy the highs. For your own sake, don't leave this until it is too late, and your world is falling apart.

We speak from direct experience; all our sons have served in the UK military. They are all damaged to varying degrees in one way or the other as a result of front line service in Iraq and Afghanistan.

Our sons, at some point, have needed help, support, and the love of their family as they muddle through life, and they try and make sense of what they have experienced as young men.

We take pride in the duty and sacrifice our sons have made in the service of there country. We do our utmost, and will continue for as long as needed to be a small part of their future support network—*We will always be there to help pick them up when they stumble and fall.*

So, always try to be the person who steps forward, not the one who shies or walks away. Be that good samaritan who knows one day it might be you or your loved ones in need!

It's about equipping you and the people around you with the tools and courage to face life and understanding how good life is, or can be.

If you can fill the unforgiving minute
With sixty seconds' worth of distance run,
Yours is the Earth and everything that's in it,
And - which is more - you'll be a Man, my son~Rudyard Kipling, If.

Always be that friend.

ACKNOWLEDGMENTS

Dad, thank you for the many inspirational quotes that you have used all your life. I have "stolen with pride." Also, for your sound and timely advice about not being big-headed or boastful when writing this book as that was never my intention when setting out on this journey.

Antti and Tomi, for some great words of wisdom. This advice changed my whole direction of travel. Jeanette's comments are insightful and compelling, and if we hadn't had our discussion, I would have completely missed this opportunity.

To my friends from many countries who I have continually pestered to give constructive comments and feedback, thank you all, you know who you are. I am very grateful for your honesty, advice, and friendship.

Thank you to my company and boss for allowing me to write and publish this book – my sincere hope is you will find this useful in developing "Key Potentials" in the future.

Thank you to Ian McHale, a respected author who helped spark my thoughts, and interest about this book, as well as helping me along my journey.

Finally, thank you, Jeanette, after a bit of gentle persuasion, she finally agreed to co-write our book, and her insight has been invaluable. She gives an honest assessment of how our success impacted on her and our family. She truly is the most amazing, giving, and unselfish person I know.

BE A SUCCESS

Why leave your success to luck, chance, or someone else.

Take control of your destiny, and turn your thoughts and dreams into reality.

You want to significantly increase your salary, job satisfaction, and work-life balance, but you're not sure what to do next.

This hands-on book written by Stephen and Jeanette McNamara will give you practical, real-life guidance on how to achieve the success you want and highlight the pitfalls and hurdles you will encounter along the way.

Don't waste your talent.

Stop dreaming and start doing.

Take the opportunity to learn from someone else's past mistakes and successes – fast track your way to what YOU want in life.